EDITOR'S NOTE

Adi Shankara's writing in Sanskrit was abstruse and esoteric. I have edited and translated his work with a view to making it easier for the reader to grasp his philosophy, commentaries and devotional poetry. My hope is that readers who enjoy this book will be led to read Shankara's work in its original and unabridged form, the better to appreciate the flow, beauty and depth of his ideas and words.

£ 8.95

'YOU
ARE THE
SUPREME
LIGHT'

'YOU ARE THE SUPREME LIGHT'

~

LIFE LESSONS FROM
ADI SHANKARA

EDITED BY

Nanditha Krishna

ALEPH

ALEPH

ALEPH BOOK COMPANY
An independent publishing firm
promoted by *Rupa Publications India*

First published in India in 2018
by Aleph Book Company
7/16 Ansari Road, Daryaganj
New Delhi 110 002

ISBN: 978-93-87561-38-0

1 3 5 7 9 10 8 6 4 2

Printed by Parksons Graphics Pvt. Ltd., Mumbai

SERIES INTRODUCTION

India has produced some of the world's greatest religious leaders, sages, saints, philosophers and spiritual thinkers. They were monks, nuns and renunciates, nationalists and reformers. No one religion had a monopoly on them. They range from Mahavira and Buddha, who lived over 2,500 years ago, to medieval saints like Chishti, Avvaiyar and Guru Nanak, to more recent philosophers and religious icons such as Vivekananda, Ramakrishna, Saint Teresa and many others. Each of them touched the lives of the people they lived among and the generations that followed. They inspired devotees and followers with their erudition and wisdom. The spiritual and philosophical heritage they left behind is India's gift to all Indians and the world.

Through the 'Life Lessons' series we will examine the teachings of some of India's best-known spiritual teachers. Each book will be a handy companion to help the reader along the difficult pathways of life.

Happiness and sorrow are unavoidable. The world is a place of trials and problems recur in every generation. Is suffering a necessary part of human life? How can one overcome suffering? Can hardship make a person stronger? What is happiness? Everybody wants to be happy, but how does one achieve this state? Does happiness come from vast riches and great achievements or does it come from the satisfaction of the soul? Is worldly success more important or is it fulfilment that one should seek?

These and similar questions vex every individual and have preoccupied the minds of philosophers and religious savants down the ages. The answers that these great souls found to life's conundrums occupy entire libraries worth of books and texts. This series is culled from their essential teachings and will present to readers some of the greatest truths to be found in India's spiritual heritage in a simple and accessible way. It is to be hoped that what you find here will prompt you to go deeper into the life and work of those who plumbed life's greatest mysteries.

Walking in the footsteps of these great men and women can take each of us to greater heights of knowledge, wisdom and understanding. They can teach us how to find happiness and peace and the true meaning of wellbeing and success. Most of all, they can teach us how to value one another and cherish the holy gift of life.

INTRODUCTION

Adi Shankara is an eighth-century philosopher best known for his doctrine of Advaita Vedanta, an important school of Hindu philosophy. He is called Adi (first) Shankara or Adi Shankaracharya (Shankara the teacher) because he was the first of many gurus, all of whom were and still are known as Shankaracharya. Vedanta is one of the six orthodox schools of Hindu philosophy that emerged from the philosophies contained in the Upanishads. Advaita, as Shankara expounded it, explains the unity of the Soul (Atman) with the Supreme Being (Brahman). He is also credited with having synthesized the various sub-sects of Hinduism—the worship of Shiva or Vishnu or Shakti or Ganesha or Surya or Skanda —that existed in the eighth century, which gave him

1

the title of Shanmata Sthapana Acharya. He sought to uphold the truths propounded by the Bhagavad Gita, Brahmasutras and the Upanishads through his commentaries.

When did Shankara live? There is no concrete answer. There is an astronomical date corresponding to the date maintained by the mathas, which is 509 BCE. There is the modern historical date of 788 CE, which doesn't have enough historical evidence to support it. All we know is that the Buddha, who probably lived between 558 and 491 BCE, preceded Shankara. There is evidence that Shankara visited Kanchipuram in the eighth century, during the reign of King Rajasimha Pallava (700–728 CE) and suggested that he should build a temple to a more gentle form of Kali as Kamakshi. Shankara also refers to the Tamil poet Thirugnana Sambandar, who lived in the seventh century CE. So it seems most likely that he lived in the eighth century. Shankara lived in a period when Sanskrit was still the lingua franca. It was a period of great spiritual churning. By Shankara's time, the Buddhist approach, which was not based on Vedic rituals and traditions, had ceased to appeal to the vast majority of Indians. Vedic sacrifices too had lost their importance and temple worship was becoming popular.

Adi Shankara rapidly gained a following because he combined in himself the artistry of a poet, the sharp intellect of a logician, the devotion of a bhakta and the intuition of a mystic, besides being the protagonist of Advaita. He was an inspired poet who appealed to every human feeling and sentiment. His descriptions of nature and his appraisal of human and divine personality were the summit of art.

Shankara travelled from his hometown Kaladi in Kerala all the way to Kashmir—teaching Advaita wherever he went. He composed poetry in praise of the towns and temples he visited. He debated with the great philosophers of the time and gained many followers and disciples on his travels. He is most famous for having set up the Shankara mathas all over the country.

Shankara spent his life wandering around India as a sanyasi, transcending distinctions of caste, teaching and preaching Vedanta. He attracted huge crowds and held discussions with eminent pandits. He never discredited his opponents and conceded whatever was acceptable to him in their school of thought. But on the vital point of Advaita he was unyielding and held his ground with his clear and incisive logic, reinforced by Vedantic texts. Yet he searched for common ground with other philosophies.

Adi Shankara was born to a Namboodri couple—Sivaguru and Aryambal—in Kaladi, modern Kerala, in the eighth century CE. Sivaguru was working as a priest in the Vadakkunathan Temple at Trichur when Shankara was born. He died when Shankara was a child, but before he died he had a vision in which he saw a glorious future for his son.

Shankara's early life was dotted with miracles. As a brahmachari* in Kaladi, he undertook the practice

---

*The first stage of a person's life—brahmacharya—was one of a student; the second stage was that of a grihastha or householder; the third was vanaprastha—retiring from a householder's responsibilities and the last was sanyasa—the spiritual stage. A brahmachari is a student.

of bhiksha, a tradition of begging for alms, which is required of any student in order to learn self-effacement and to conquer the ego. At one of the houses, the woman of the house gave him a small ripe amla (Indian gooseberry), as that was all she could offer. Moved by her kindness even in her straitened circumstances, Shankara composed and recited the Kanakadhara Stotram (Hymn Causing the Flow of Gold), praying to Goddess Lakshmi to shower wealth on the kind lady. This was probably Shankara's first composition. Following his prayer, there was a shower of gold on the house. The house, known as Suvarnakattu Mana (the golden house), still exists in Kaladi and the local people believe that its wealth was the result of divine intervention because of the hymn.

Shankara completed his Vedic education and Sanskrit studies at a very young age and wanted to become a sanyasi. But his mother did not wish to lose her only son who was the solace of her widowhood and old age. One day, when Shankara and his mother were bathing in the Poorna River, a crocodile attacked and grabbed hold of Shankara's foot. Shankara begged his mother to give him permission to assume sanyas, failing which he was in imminent danger of death. When the reluctant mother gave her consent to save her son's life, the crocodile released Shankara. He could now become a sanyasi and leave Kaladi in search of a guru. Thus began Shankara's peripatetic life.

While Shankara had learnt the scriptures, he needed a teacher who could take him further on his philosophical journey. He reached the banks of the Narmada River where he met Govinda Bhagavatpada who had written the famous karika (meaning) of the Mandukya Upanishad. Shankara became his disciple and completed his apprenticeship by the age of sixteen, learning the Vedas, Upanishads and Brahmasutras. Thereafter, he left for Benares (also known as Kashi and Varanasi) to expound the teachings of Vedanta.

In Benares, Shankara attracted crowds of people who wished to listen to his exposition of Vedanta. It was at this time that he wrote his commentaries on the Gita, Upanishads and Brahmasutras. These expositions were studied by his students, the most famous of whom was Padmapada, originally Vishnu

Sharma or Sanandana. It was here that Shankara was conferred the title of acharya or teacher.

Shankara soon started meeting several learned gurus and engaging in debates with them. A significant encounter was with a Chandala (as those beyond the pale of caste were then referred to). On coming across a Chandala couple in his path, he asked them to move out of the way. As per the custom of the times, outcastes were not permitted to come in the way of an upper-caste person as their presence was considered polluting. The Chandala responded: 'Do you want the body made up of food to move away from another body made up of food? Or do you want consciousness to move away from consciousness?' In other words, who should move—the body or the soul? Shankara, amazed at his wisdom and superior understanding, fell at the feet of the Chandala. In response, Shankara composed the famous *Manisha Panchakam*, a hymn that rejects the caste system and reiterates that we all are one. The few verses of this poem contain the essence of Vedantic teaching and an enunciation of the ultimate unity of the Universe that must lead to acceptance and infinite comprehension.

One of his most famous encounters was with Mandana Mishra, the great exponent of Poorva Mimamsa, the earliest school of philosophy, at Mahishmati (in modern Madhya Pradesh). Mimamsa belief is that our existence in the material world is endless—there is no liberation or moksha. The cycle of karma is perpetual, and one can only aim for a higher birth among the Devas or Gods (like Shiva, Vishnu, etc.) Therefore, the purpose of the Vedas is to perform rituals for achieving good karma. Shankara wanted to meet Kumarila Bhatta, a famous exponent of Mimamsa, but the latter was at the end of his life. Bhatta recommended that Shankara meet his brother-in-law, Mandana Mishra. The two debated over eighteen days, with Mishra's wife, Ubhaya Bharati, appointed as umpire. Finally, Mishra acknowledged defeat and, in his wife's presence, renounced his life as a householder and took sanyas. Mandana Mishra became Shankara's second great disciple. He was renamed Sureshwaracharya, and later became the first head of the Sringeri matha, now in Karnataka.

Shankara's ability to win over Mishra was a tremendous achievement and led to a synthesis of the Advaita and Vedic schools.

An apocryphal story is inserted into the debate with Mandana Mishra. His wife, Ubhaya Bharati, also known as Sarasavani, insisted on continuing the debate as she was one-half of Mandana Mishra, being his wife. A reluctant Shankara was forced to agree. She asked him questions on kama and sex which he knew nothing about. He asked for a month's time to learn, left his body in a cave beside the Narmada and entered the dead body of King Amaruka by parakaya pravesha (transmigration of the soul into another body). After a month in the king's palace and harem, he returned and defeated Ubhaya Bharati in debate.

Shankara contended that the Mimamsakas were wrong and that karma marga (path of ritual action) was not the only correct path to knowledge. The jnana marga (path of realization) was the superior way, he said, but added that the Vedas had two parts—karma marga and jnana marga—and both were valid, but they resulted in different outcomes. Those who did not wish to find self-realization could choose the path of rituals. By preaching that both karma marga and jnana marga were valid, he was able to fill the vacuum that the Buddhists, who rejected both the Supreme Being and rituals, were unable to fill, and thus the Vedic religion gradually overcame Buddhism, which was already in a state of decline by the Gupta period (fourth to sixth centuries CE).

During his travels, Shankara received a message that his mother was ill. He rushed back to be at her bedside before she passed away. There is a story about his mother's funeral rites, which is most likely apocryphal. As Shankara was a sanyasi, he had essentially given up all ties to his family and was not allowed to conduct any of the ceremonies associated with her death. He requested the assistance of the villagers to help him cremate her body. But the orthodoxy was unyielding, saying that a sanyasi who had given up the conventional observance of religious rites could not perform his mother's funeral. Shankara made a funeral pyre out of plantain stalks and cremated her in a corner of the compound of his house. Thereafter, the local ruler passed an order that henceforth all Namboodris would have a similar funeral.

As Shankara continued his travels around the country, he gained many disciples and installed them as heads of the mathas he established throughout the country. He established mathas at:

Dwarka—Paschimnaya Shri Sharada Peetham or Kalika Matha;

Badrinath—Uttaramnaya Shri Jyotish Peetham or Jyotir Matha;

Puri—Pooramnaya Shri Govardhana Peetham

Sringeri—Dakshinamnaya Shri Sringeri Sharada Peetham; and

Kanchipuram—Dakshinamnaya Kanchi Kamakoti Peetham.

Mandana Mishra, as Sureshwaracharya, became the first head of the Sringeri Sharada peetham and was also put in charge of the Kanchi Kamakoti peetham. Hastamalaka was the first acharya of the Kalika matha in Dwarka. Totakacharya was the first head of the Jyotir matha in Badrinath, about thirty kilometres from the temple of Shri Badrinath, near the Alakananda River. Padmapada was the first acharya of the Puri matha. They were all given the title 'Shankaracharya', for they followed the Advaita Vedanta propagated by Adi Shankara. It was not only Brahmins who could become Shankaracharyas. Over the years, people of other castes, including a Jain, have become Shankaracharyas. The mathas have preserved the teachings of Shankara and the continuing influence of Adi Shankara is probably due to the institutionalization of his teachings. The acharyas of the Shankara mathas must be sanyasis or renunciates, in keeping with Adi Shankara's philosophy of rejection of the material world and Advaita or non-duality.

A major contribution of Shankara to the Vedic ritual was the abolition of animal—and probably human—sacrifice wherever he went. At Kanchipuram, not only did he stop sacrifices at the famous temple of Kamakshi, he also persuaded the king to build a new temple with a soumya (pacific) image of the Goddess, as against the earlier roudra (angry) image of Kalikambal with three severed heads beneath her folded leg and a skull in one hand. He stopped animal sacrifice in the Pashupatinath Temple at Nepal and the Brahma Chamundi Temple in Chidambaram, Tamil Nadu, and many other temples all over India.

Shankara visited the Sharada peeth in Kashmir, now an abandoned temple located in the village of Sharda on the Neelam River in Pakistan-occupied Kashmir. Sharada peeth was a great centre of learning, and one of the eighteen Shakti peethas, which were important shrines and pilgrimage centres of the Shakti cult. In 1030 CE, the Persian scholar and historian Al Biruni visited Kashmir and reported seeing a wooden idol of Sharada Devi in the temple, which was later destroyed by marauding Islamic armies in the fourteenth century. Kashmir was once called Sharada Desh after this temple and Sharada Devi was called Kashmira Puravasini. Sharada is also a native script of Kashmir.

At Sharada peeth in Kashmir, Adi Shankara was given the right to sit at the Sarva jnana (or Sarvajna) peetham (throne of wisdom). The first verse of

Prapanchasaara composed by Adi Shankara is in praise of goddess Sharada Devi. The original wooden idol of Sharada Devi at the Sringeri Sharada peetham in Karnataka is supposed to have been brought to the south from Kashmir by Adi Shankara. Shankara, an ardent devotee of Shakti, installed the Shri chakra or yantra—mystical Tantric diagrams worshipped in temples and homes with supposed occult powers— wherever he went. According to his student, Madhava, Shankara consecrated a Shri Chakra—believed to have been given to him by Lord Shiva himself in Badrinath—in the temple of Bhagavati or Kamakshi in Kanchipuram (in the original temple of Kalikambal or Adi Kamakshi). His worship of Shakti was probably influenced by his childhood years in Kerala, where the Tantric worship of Bhagavati and the Sri Chakra is still very popular.

In spite of his espousal of a single Supreme Being, Shankara composed beautiful poetry to the deities of the Shanmata, the six schools of Hinduism. His *Shivananda Lahari* is a beautiful outpouring to Lord Shiva, whom he identifies with the Supreme Being:

Let one live in a cave, in a house, in the
forest, on top of a mountain,
In water or fire, of what use is such a life?
O Shambho, if a person's mind remains at
your feet,
that, in truth, is yoga. He is the supreme
yogin, the one who is most happy.

And Shiva is the protector of the poor:
Oh Shiva, the Pure One. Let Brahma live
long. Let his four heads be protected by you.
For he has decreed for me poverty in this
world. But what anxiety can I have
when your kind glance, which is always
turned towards the poor will,
of its own accord, protect me?

Shankara died at the age of thirty-two. Towards the
end of his life, Shankara travelled to Assam, to the
home of someone who belonged to the Tantra cult.
Here he fell very ill. Yet he managed to travel to
Kedarnath as he wanted to spend his final days there.

It is believed that Shankara gave up his life as he was chanting Aham Brahmasmi (I am Brahman or I am Divine)—one of the tenets of the Advaita philosophy that he expounded.

Shankara was unarguably one of the greatest men who ever walked this land. Possessed of a brilliant mind, his ideas, thought process, analyses, compositions and achievements at the young age of thirty-two are stupendous. If the British claim they created India, they need to be reminded of this young man who walked the length and breadth of the subcontinent over a thousand years ago, marking the four directions by four mathas: Badrinath in the north, Sringeri and Kanchipuram in the south, Puri in the east and Dwarka in the west.

THE PHILOSOPHY OF ADI SHANKARA

Adi Shankara was unique, combining in himself poet, logistician, debater, devotee and mystic, besides being the architect of the Advaita school of philosophy. Within a short period of thirty odd years, Shankara demonstrated a marvellous capacity for organization, by establishing mathas in the north, south, east and west, devoted to the continuation of the doctrines he had expounded in his life. He united the subcontinent by appointing a disciple from one part of the country in another. The first heads of the mathas were his first students, sanyasis who dedicated their lives to the efficacy and practicability of Advaita, thereby ensuring its continuity. His mathas live on to this day, providing spiritual guidance for Hindus, although they have become a new orthodoxy, something that Adi Shankara rejected all his life.

Shankara's achievements in his short life were many. He rejected caste (see *Manisha Panchakam* and *Dasha shloki*), sub-sects, rituals, and animal sacrifice. He united Hindus and Hinduism by unifying the various sects under a single Brahman or Supreme Soul, who manifested Himself in various forms. He brought Buddhism back into the Hindu fold by claiming the Buddha as an incarnation of Vishnu. After all, the Buddha always reiterated the importance of the Vedas and had not rejected them. He was merely against sacrifice and preached compassion. Shankara established Shankara mathas led by learned teachers who could give philosophical guidance to the people.

Adi Shankara firmly established the philosophy of Advaita or non-duality, which has been described as one of the supreme achievements of Hinduism. His teachings are contained in his commentaries on the Bhagavad Gita, Upanishads and Brahmasutras and in such condensed expositions as *Viveka Chudamani*, *Atmabodha*, *Shata shloki*, *Prabodha sudhakara*, *Aparokshanubhuti* and that unequalled compendium of wisdom, the *Dakshinamurti Stotram*. In his commentaries, Adi Shankara displayed the rare ability of relentlessly logical argument and built up a reputation for subtle reasoning, which has not been surpassed in any philosophical writings since then. The main features of his philosophy are the affirmation of samsara, or the succession of births and deaths conditioned by karma, and its cosmic significance; the realization of the essential relativity of phenomena in the context of the unchanging reality of the Supreme Soul (the Absolute or Brahman); and the understanding that truth is not theoretical but is in fact a direct realization and actual experience, which is summarized in the words 'Tat tvam asi' (Thou art that). It signifies the absolute equality of the Supreme Being (Tat) with the individual soul (tvam).

According to Adi Shankara, we see diversity where there is unity and many where there is one because of ignorance. The Supreme Being or Brahman is indivisible, all-pervading, without attributes (nirguna) and One. The individual soul or Atman is identical with the Supreme Being. While the world of phenomena is relatively real, Brahman is the only eternal reality at a metaphysical level. Shankara was unique in his insistence on knowledge by investigation and not by the mere acceptance of assertions by others. He did not accept blind faith, which is generally propounded by most religions.

He was, simultaneously, the author of beautiful poetry like the *Soundarya Lahari*, devoted to the adoration of a personal Godhead in several manifestations; the *Atma Shatakam*, where he defines the Supreme Soul or the Absolute; *Bhaja Govindam*, in adoration of the Lord; and *Kanakadhara Stotram*, in praise of Goddess Lakshmi. In the *Dakshinamurti Stotram*, he invokes the Supreme Being as the embodiment of earth, water, fire, air, ether, the sun, moon and soul; one who is supreme and all-pervading; and beyond whom there exists nothing for the seeker. In his *Soundarya Lahari* he invokes the Mother Goddess: 'Whatever I articulate may be prayer and whatever act I perform may be your worship'.

He summarized his teachings in four sentences taken from the Upanishads, known as the Mahavakyas:

Aham Brahmasmi—I am Brahman or I am Divine (Aitareya Upanishad 3.3);

Ayam atma Brahma—This Soul in Brahman (Mandukya Upanishad 1.2);

Tat tvam asi—Thou art that (Chandogya Upanishad 6.8.7); and

Prajnyanam Brahma—Knowledge is Brahman (Aitareya Upanishad 3.3).

There is considerable misunderstanding regarding the

real meaning of Shankara's Advaita. He asserts that the eternal, Brahman (the Supreme or Absolute Being) is the only Ultimate Reality. He explains that the experience of various phenomena of the Universe is due to the power of maya, by which the Absolute, without undergoing any change, appears as an ever-changing succession of phenomena conditioned by time and space. The spirit of man, said Shankara, is identical to the Supreme Being and our sufferings and errors are due to our failure to realize this oneness. He who has achieved this realization can attain moksha or liberation. One of his chief doctrines is that karma (work) and upasana (worship) are ancillary to jnana (knowledge or illumination).

Shankara's conception of the Absolute is not a mere matter of intellectual subtlety. According to him, the relation of Brahman (the Supreme Being) to the world is impossible to explain (anirvachaneeya). Brahman is without attributes and unchanging. Ishvara, the Saguna (with form), is himself a product of maya, being the nearest version of the Nirguna (formless) Brahman that is possible for the individual soul to imagine. The world is the apparent transformation through maya of the Nirguna Brahman. Jiva, the Supreme Soul, is, in reality, all-pervading and identical with Brahman. When the Jiva is broken into individual souls by its upadhis or adjuncts, the Jiva regards itself as a doer or an agent.

It is wrong to say that Shankara said that the world was unreal or a figment of illusion. In fact, he was at pains to point out that the idea of unreality was a part of the Buddhist (yogachara) doctrine. Adi Shankara describes maya thus: 'Man's senses may deceive him; his memory may play him false; the forms of the world may be a matter of delusion; the objects of knowledge or perception may be doubted; but the doubter himself cannot be doubted.' This position leads to the conclusion that the Soul, which is composed of Consciousness and Bliss (Sachchitananda), is universal and infinite, whereas the world of objects is subject to mutation. In other words, the world, as perceived, is as real as the perceiver. In saying this, Shankara differs from the yogachara teachings of Buddhism.

The world, according to Shankara, is neither non-existing nor void. Its attributes are neither non-existent (abhava) nor nothing (shunya). But it is not the Ultimate Reality either and this is where our confusion arises, because we do not differentiate between the basic Soul (Atman) and impermanence (anatman). Moksha is achieved when the Supreme Truth is realized. It is not nirvana in the sense of dissolution, but the replacement of ignorance (avidya) by self-realization (vidya). In the *Viveka Chudamani*, Shankara says that deliverance is not achieved by repeating the word Brahman but by directly experiencing Brahman.

Shankara then expounds the idea that the Absolute becomes abstract (nirakar) for the individual worshipper as a personal God or Saguna Brahman, which is the only form in which the Absolute can be comprehended by the human mind. The religion of a personal God is not a mere dogma, but is a product of realization and experience. Bhakti is realization leading to unification with a personal God or symbol, which may be an image, a painting or an object in nature.

Thus Shankara does not exclude the framework of the external world. This is an aspect that is not always understood by commentators on Vedanta.

The Supreme Being or Brahman may be mentally or intellectually envisaged. But there is also a deep-rooted desire for personal separateness, which is ignorance or avidya and the play of maya. It creates the notion in the worshipper that he is the actor; he is the one who experiences. This notion is the cause of bondage to existence—birth, death and rebirth—and this notion can be removed only by a strenuous effort to live in union with the Brahman. Such eradication is called moksha. Shankara stated that when a man follows the ways of the world, or even the way of tradition (i.e. when he believes in religious rites and in the scriptures), he cannot attain knowledge of reality—it can only be achieved when the seeker attains knowledge (jnana).

The entire universe consisting of namaroopa or 'names and forms', said Shankara, is but an appearance and Brahman is the sole reality. Its attainment and the annihilation of maya, or the great illusion of the

Universe, by a process of self-realization, were the objects of his life.

The ideals of Shankara pervaded and influenced not only all aspects of Indian thought, but has had significant echoes amongst Sufi divines, medieval Christian saints, and more recent thinkers. There is, furthermore, a growing body of scientific thinkers who, confronted by the developments of nuclear, atomic and cosmic theories, feel irresistibly drawn to Shankara's enunciations as the most legitimate and satisfactory explanation of the Universe, physical, psychological and para-psychological. The more one studies the teachings of Shankara and his source books, the Upanishads, Brahmasutra and Bhagavad Gita, the more one is struck by the intuition and anticipation of past seers of what are now coming to be regarded as scientific truths. Atomic theory and the existence of a reservoir of incalculable energy in atoms, the doctrine of conservation of energy and many of the developments of physics, chemistry and biology regarding the potential of the infinitesimally small and the infinitely great, are all demonstrated as evolutionary products and transmutations of primal energy. Life (prana) is a continuous vibration or manifestation of energy.

Shankara was not without his critics. The twelfth-century *Padma Purana* is a text that attacks Shankara and his doctrines. The description 'crypto Buddhist' (prachchanna boudha) was applied to Shankara in a passage where Lord Shiva is supposed to have declared to Devi that the theory of maya is a false doctrine, a disguised form of Buddhism. However, this purana is strongly Vaishnavite, with Shiva explaining to Parvati the nature and attributes of Vishnu whom they both join in praising and adoring. The *Padma Purana* reveals a common misconception regarding both Shankara and the Buddha. Critics forget that both the great seers freely and openly took their ideas from the early Upanishads, although they developed their teachings differently. The main background of Shankara's philosophy is based on the Mandukyopanishad, on which Shankara composed his well-known commentary. The only common feature between Gautama Buddha and Adi Shankara was the rejection by both of narrow theological obsessions. In addition, Shankara included the Buddha among the incarnations of Vishnu, a bold and innovative step to assimilate the great preacher, put forward the Buddhist view and finally to demolish it by making Buddha an incarnation of Lord Vishnu. Now Buddhism was absorbed into Sanatana Dharma. He admired Buddha's compassion and his philosophy of Advaita. 'I worship that spiritual radiance which manifested as the Buddha, who was all-knowing, the conqueror of maya, who was full of mercy and who was adored by those who were opposed to the performance of (animal) sacrifices,' said Adi Shankara.

The special achievement of Shankara is that, apart from being a protagonist of monism, he is the author of innumerable devotional hymns. The realization (jnana) advocated by Shankara was a warm-hearted quest for the truth, which, when turned towards a personal deity, became bhakti or devotion.

Shankara, while accepting the Mimamsa rules of interpretation, regarded the Vedas as explanatory, revealing truths, but not as mandatory. According to

Shankara, the test of the authority of a passage was its capacity to generate fruitful knowledge.

Adi Shankara was a revolutionary, no less than the Buddha, and emphasized the importance of compassion and an ethical life. While the Buddha's teachings were also drawn from the Upanishads, their adoption by later rulers resulted in the rejection of several Vedic traditions. Shankara, on the other hand, was inclusive and a synthesizer, even while he too rejected much of what the Buddha rejected, like rituals and animal sacrifice. Shankara was as insistent as the Buddha on the supreme importance of ethics as one of the fundamentals of spiritual life, but his outlook on karma, temple worship and domestic ceremonies was sympathetic and harmonious with the Vedic view.

During his lifetime, Hinduism as we know it today, or rather Sanatana Dharma, was a mix of religious and philosophical ideas ranging from the Vedas to simple village deities. There was no unity in this multitude of cults. Shankara established the six forms of religious worship, for which he was known as the Shanmata Sthapana Acharya, or 'the teacher who established the six religions'. At that time there were six major deities—Shiva, Vishnu, Shakti, Surya, Ganesha and Kartikeya—with followers who were busy quarrelling with each other, claiming the superiority of their chosen deity. Adi Shankara brought together these quarrelling sects by integrating the worship of these deities beneath the Nirguna Brahman, the single divine power, the Supreme Being. They are but reflections of one Saguna Brahman, or a personal God with attributes, said Adi Shankara. With his philosophy of Advaita, Shankara combined the Shanmata or 'six religions' within one Supreme Brahman with six manifestations. His philosophy is not as sectarian as either Vaishnavism or Shaivism and is based on the recognition that Brahman is the highest principle in the universe, which pervades all of existence. His philosophy is followed even today by the Smarthas, who accept all the major Hindu Gods and follow a philosophical path of meditation, emphasizing man's oneness with God.

The number and depth of Adi Shankara's

compositions are unbelievable for a man who composed between the ages of eight and thirty-two. His works include:

Devotional hymns to the Gods: Ganesha, Subrahmanya, Shiva, Devi, Vishnu, Lakshmi and Hanuman.

Devotional hymns to cities and rivers: Kashi, Jyotirlingam, Ganga, Narmada, Yamuna, Pushkar* ashtakam.

Prakarna granthas (basic Vedantic texts)

Bhashya granthas (commentaries): Vishnu Sahasranamam, Lalita Trishati, Yogasutras, Bhagavad Gita, the Principal Upanishads and the Brahmasutras.

In his life span of thirty-two years Adi Shankara travelled throughout India, established the doctrine of Vedanta, participated in debates lasting several days with strangers in strange places. His followers

---

*Pushkaram is a festival celebrated in shrines along the banks of the major sacred rivers, with spiritual discourses, devotional music and cultural programmes.

were legion, belonging to every part of the country. His genius and his marvellously analytical intellect affected the whole subcontinent without the aid of any medium to propagate his ideas except himself. Not only did he preach the doctrines of Vedanta, which could even sound nihilistic, but he also composed exquisite poetry with luscious images of nature and great intuition. He evolved from a many-sided devotee to a devastating critic of pretentiousness, foolishness and blind faith. In one of his songs to Shiva he prays that he may be saved from the life of a priest, from leading a disreputable life, from becoming a local leader or pontiff, from being a witness in a court of law and, finally, from being a liar, arrogant or lacking in mercy.

Shankara destroyed the distinction between the individual soul and the Supreme Soul. He destroyed many dogmas, but was very catholic in his outlook. He was not merely a 'dreaming idealist but a practical visionary'. The ultimate source of inspiration is one, although the truth may be interpreted variously and applied differently to different people. The Supreme

Being can only be described as 'Not this', 'Not that' (Neti neti).

WHO AM I?

When Adi Shankara, as a young boy of eight, was wandering around near the Narmada River in search of his guru, he met the sage Govinda Bhagavatpada, who asked him who he was. Shankara answered him in six stanzas, known as *Atma Shatakam* or *Nirvana Shatakam*. The sage recognized the brilliance of Adi Shankara and accepted him as his disciple.

Atman means the Soul, the Supreme Soul or Brahman, while nirvana means an idyllic state or liberation. This poem describes the Atman according to Adi Shankara's philosophy of Advaita or non-dualism, whereby the individual soul is a part of the Supreme Being.

I am neither the mind, nor the intelligence,
nor the ego, nor the reflection
of the inner self,
I am not the organs of hearing,
taste, smell, or vision,
I am not the sky, earth, fire or air,
I am the ever pure blissful consciousness;
I am auspicious, I am Shiva.

I am not the vital breath, nor the
five vital airs,
I am not the seven essential elements (of the
body), nor the five sheaths (of the body),
I am not the organ of speech, touch,
movement, procreation or elimination,
I am the ever pure blissful consciousness;
I am auspicious, I am Shiva.

I have no hatred, no dislike, no attachment,
greed or infatuation,
I have no pride, or envy, or jealousy,
I am not bound by righteousness, wealth,

desire or liberation,
I am the ever pure blissful consciousness;
I am auspicious, I am Shiva.

I am not bound by merits or sins, nor by
happiness or sorrow,
nor am I bound by sacred hymns or sacred
places, sacred scriptures or rituals,
I am neither enjoyment, nor an object to be
enjoyed, nor the enjoyer,
I am the ever pure blissful consciousness;
I am auspicious, I am Shiva.

I am not bound by death or fear of it,
nor by the rules of birth,
caste and its distinctions,
I have no father or mother, I have no birth,
I have no relations, no friends,
no guru, or disciple,
I am the ever pure blissful consciousness;
I am auspicious, I am Shiva.

I am all pervasive, and without any attributes
or form,
I am not attached to the world
or to liberation,
I am everywhere, everything, every time,
I am the ever pure blissful consciousness;
I am auspicious, I am Shiva.

I AM A PART OF YOU

At the sacred city of Varanasi, Adi Shankara was going to the temple after his bath. On the way, he saw an outcaste couple in his path and, as was the custom in those days, asked them to move away. To his utter amazement, the outcaste replied, 'O great sage, tell me, when you say go away, taking me to be an outcaste, is your body addressing another body or is one soul addressing another? Which, O sage, do you wish should go away?' Adi Shankara immediately fell at the feet of the outcaste, deeming the couple to be Lord Shiva and his consort Parvati, and composed the *Manisha Panchakam* (Five Verses of Conviction).

Doesn't the sun shine both on the sacred
Ganga and on the cesspools in the dirty lanes?

Is there any difference whether the reflection
of the sky is seen in a container
made of gold or of clay?

The Universe is assumed to consist of diverse
and different things.
He who firmly believes in this
unity in diversity,
he is my teacher, irrespective of whether he is
a Brahmin or an outcaste.

He is a great master, be he a Brahmin or
an outcaste who, dwelling on the pure and
infinite Supreme Being, thinks of himself as
a part of that very Being.

The differences in our physical bodies are the
products of our previous deeds,
good and bad, pertaining to our past, present
and future lives.
The one who reduces the sins to ashes in the

flaming fire of knowledge
is the best informed.

The Supreme Being is within all animals,
people and the gods themselves.
It is by the reflection of this Being that the
mind, body and senses are sentient.
But the Supreme Being within us is
concealed by the mind, senses and body,
just as the sun is hidden by the clouds.
The person who, with perfect understanding
and wisdom,
always meditates on the Supreme Being
alone,
he is my teacher.

He whose mind is united with the
Supreme Being
and is at great peace is
not merely a knower of Brahman but is
Brahman itself.
Such a person, whoever he may be, is fit to

be worshipped by the gods.
O Lord, in the form of this body,
I am your servant.
In the form of life, I am a part of you.
In the form of soul, you are within me and
in every other being or animal that I behold.

YOU ARE THE SUPREME LIGHT

Shankaracharya successfully summarized the essence of Advaita in one verse called *Eka shloki* (single shloka). It is a dialogue between a teacher and student, in response to a question by the student on self-realization.

Teacher: How do you see?
Student: I see with the help of sunlight.
Teacher: How do you see in the night?
Student: I see by the light of a lamp.
Teacher: How do you see the light? How do you see even before you open your eyes?
Student: I see with my intellect.
Teacher: What helps you see that intellect?

Student: It is I.

Teacher: Then, you are that Supreme Light.

Student: I realize that I am.

TWELVE BLOSSOMS

Adi Shankara was walking along a street in Kashi, accompanied by his fourteen disciples when he heard the sound of a man teaching grammatical rules. He followed the voice, which led him to an elderly scholar who was teaching his students. He told the scholar to forget grammar and instead to 'Adore the Lord, O fool! When it is time to leave this world, the repetition of grammar rules will not help you'.

Adi Shankara composed twelve stanzas, known as *Dvadasha Manjarika Stotra* (Hymn of Twelve Blossoms). His fourteen disciples added one stanza each, called a hymn of fourteen blossoms (*Chaturdasha Manjarika Stotra*). Strung together, the hymn is titled *Bhaja Govindam*, or the Hymn to Govinda. Although he was an ardent devotee of Shiva and Shakti, he had no hesitation in composing a poem in honour of Krishna. The sectarian divide was to come two hundred years later.

The great Carnatic vocalist, the late M. S. Subbulakshmi, set this poem to beautiful music.

Give up your insatiable desire for wealth,
be satisfied with what you have,
the fruits of your own labour.

There is no happiness from wealth.
Why, the wealthy fear even their own
children.

Who is your wife? Who is your son?
Who are you? From where have you come?
Think of that.

Life is as unstable as water on a lotus leaf.
Yet the whole world is devoured by conceit
and sorrow.

Do not be proud of your wealth, family and
youth:
Time takes them all away.
This world is an illusion, so prepare to
renounce it.
Only the mentally mature can go on the path
of renunciation.

Do not fall a prey to delusion and lust,
think carefully and control your senses.

There is no virtue in mere asceticism.
It is essential that you free yourself from
desire and attachment.

Give up desire, anger, greed and delusion,
and ask yourself, 'Who am I?'

Day and night, dusk and dawn, winter and
spring come and go.
Time passes, and life flies by.
Yet we are still in the grip of desire.

Why worry about wife and wealth
when only the company of good people
can take you across the sea of life?

There is only one God in you and me and
everyone else.
See the One everywhere
and give up the sense of difference from all
other beings.

A man may bathe in the Ganga
or in the sea,
he may be austere or give lavish gifts.
Yet all religions agree that none of these will
liberate him
if he does not acquire true knowledge.

Adi Shankara's disciples added some more stanzas.

As long as there is breath in your body,
people will ask about your welfare.
Once life has left the body,

your dependents will dread the dead body.

As a boy, one is attached to sports,
as a youth, to women,
as an old man, to anxiety.
Alas! Nobody is attached to the Supreme Being.

Through the company of good people rises
detachment.
Through detachment arises freedom from
delusion.
Without delusion rises steadfastness.
Through steadfastness arises liberation.

When youth is gone, what is the use of lust?
When water has evaporated, what is the use
of the lake?
When money has gone,
where are one's relatives?
When Truth is known,
where is the worldly bond?

The ascetic with matted locks, the man with
shaven head,
The ascetic with his hair pulled out, the
man disguised in ochre robes,
They have eyes but do not see.
They disguise themselves to cheat the world.

When the body is old and the hair is grey,
when he is toothless and has to walk with
the help of a stick,
the old man still does not lose desire.

There is a fire before him, the sun behind.
The ascetic sleeps at night with his knees
tucked beneath his chin.
He stretches out his hand for alms and lives
beneath a tree.
Yet he has not yet lost his desire.

Whether one is practising yoga or enjoying
simple pleasure,
whether in company or alone,

he alone is happy who thinks of the
Supreme Being.

Studying the Bhagavad Gita, drinking the
water of the Ganga,
and worshipping the Lord will save you from
fear of death.

Repeated birth, death and rebirth,
is an ocean that is difficult to cross.
Save me, O merciful Lord.

Clad in rags and treading a path beyond
good and evil,
the yogi revels in the Supreme Brahman.

Who are you? Who am I?
Who are my mother or father?
Think about it.
The cares and worries of the world
are a dream.
Free yourself from that dream.

Don't think: O friend or foe, son or relative,
if you want to realize the Supreme Being,
think of all as one.

Sing the Bhagavad Gita and the Thousand
Names of the Lord,
meditate on Lord Vishnu.
Be in the company of good people
and distribute wealth among the poor.

First, there is pleasure, then there is disease.
Finally comes death.
Yet men do not give up their sinful ways.

Regulate your breathing, control your senses,
discriminate between the eternal and the
transient.
Meditation and prayer
must be performed with great care.

Put your faith in your teacher
and you will be free from the cares of life.

Once your senses and mind
are under control
you will realize the God residing
in your heart.

THE SUPREME BEING

I am not the imaginary I, the ego, my name.
I am not the temporary
I, my body or my mind.
I am the everlasting Life Force,
behind all living beings.
I am the source of Universal Love
and Happiness.
Aham Brahmasmi—I am Brahman.

The Supreme Being is one and
without any attributes.
But each worshipper assigns
various attributes.
Thus are the meditations different with the
difference in the assigned attributes.

There are two types of knowledge.
Higher knowledge is knowledge of the
Supreme Being.
Lower knowledge deals with duties and
actions that must be condemned.
Lower knowledge is ignorance
and must be discarded.
When lower knowledge is gained,
Truth remains elusive.
Higher knowledge is the
realization of immortality.

The Supreme Being cannot be realized by
mere mastery over words.
A guru, and the rejection of all desire is
essential to find the Supreme Being.

Om is Brahman.
Om is also a symbol of Brahman.
By meditating on Om, the follower may
attain greater or lesser knowledge.

The Supreme Being cannot be realized
by the mind alone.
For those who meditate on Om and regard it
as a symbol of the Supreme,
the Supreme Being reveals itself.

Although there is but one Brahman
Brahman has two forms:
He is qualified by limiting conditions.
He is also free of all conditions.

The dual nature of Brahman
comes from the fact
that He is the object of either knowledge
or ignorance.

Om is a peg on which is hung
the idea of Brahman,
just as the image is for the idea of Vishnu.
Om must be meditated upon
as the sound form of the Supreme Being.

Truth, knowledge and infinity are the
characteristics of the Supreme Being.

The unreal has no existence and the real
never ceases to be.

I am neither maya nor its effect in any form,
I am consciousness, Brahman and none else.
I am eternally pure, enlightened,
free and absolute,
the Innermost Consciousness.
To remain in this state of total identification
with Brahman
is known as Samadhi.

Those realized souls who have attained
knowledge of Brahman
even after liberation
are empowered to continue to work for the
welfare of the world.

I will explain in half a shloka the substance

of crores of texts:
Brahman is real. The universe is an illusion.
The Individual Soul and the Supreme Soul
are not strangers.
They are not two different entities.

KNOWLEDGE OF TRUTH

Shankara composed prakaranas (expositions) to help the seeker comprehend the subtle themes of the scriptures. The *Tattvabodha* is a prakarna (exposition) with definitions to achieve knowledge and unity with the Supreme Being.

The Eternal is only one, and that is
Brahman. Everything else is impermanent.
Detachment is the total lack of interest in the
pleasures of this world and heaven too.
The six spiritual treasures are mind control,
sense control, mental tranquillity, endurance,
concentration and faith.

Intense desire is the desire to be liberated.

True knowledge is comprehension that the
Self is true and everything else is false.

The gross physical body is made up of
the five supreme elements that express the
experience of happiness or misery born of
past good or bad actions.
The gross body is born of five
transfigurations: birth, life, growth, change
and death. The ear, skin, eyes, tongue and
nose are the instruments of knowledge.
The five organs are the medium of actions.

The subtle body consists of the five organs of
knowledge, the five organs of action,
the five vital forces, the mind and the
intellect—the seventeen organs.

The causal body is formed from ignorance, is
ignorant of its own nature
and does not undergo any modification.

The three states of existence are waking,
dreaming and deep sleep.
The Self is identified with the
gross physical body.
All that is heard or seen in the waking state
become mental impressions.
The world that appears in the sleep state is
called the dream state.
Deep sleep is a state when you
do not know anything.

The five sheaths are food, the life-force, the
mind, knowledge and the state of bliss.

Atman or the Self is the nature
of the Supreme Being,
a state of knowledge and absolute bliss.

The three qualities of ignorance are serenity
(sattva), activity (rajas) and inertia (tamas).

The Self is the Supreme Being,
a state of consciousness and bliss.

The living being (jiva) thinks that Ishvara is
different. The ignorant Self is the jiva.

Ishvara is hidden by the falsity of maya.
As long as there is a difference between jiva
and Ishvara, birth and death will not go.
Therefore, never differentiate between jiva
and Ishvara.

Can there be no difference between the living
being with ego and limited knowledge and
the all-knowing Ishvara without ego?

Ishvara and living beings are not different as
there is no difference in Consciousness.

'Thou art that' (Tat tvam asi) is pure
Consciousness, free of all attributes.

The unattached all-pervasive Self is the
liberated-in-life (jivanmukti).

Knowing that 'I am Brahman', one is freed
from the bondage of action (karma).

There are three types of fruits of action: that
which should yield fruit in the future,
that which is stored, and that which has
begun to yield fruit.
A person can carry out actions that will
impact the future if his self-knowledge—both
good and bad—is awakened.

Sanchita karma is that which remains in the
form of a seed even after multiple births.

Praarabdha karma is that which gives birth to
this body in this world,
and makes us experience happiness
and misery.

Such karmas can only be eliminated by
experience.

Karmas can be destroyed by the
decisive knowledge
'I am Brahman' (Aham Brahmasmi).

One who knows the Self has attained
Brahman, having crossed world
lines in this life itself.
The Vedas say that one who knows the Self
transcends sorrow.
The Smritis say that one who attains
knowledge of the Supreme Being
does not care where his body falls, since he
has destroyed all desires.

I am the Self. I am everything.
I am beyond everything.
I have no other. I am Consciousness.
I am Bliss.

SELF-REALIZATION

Atmabodha, meaning 'Knowledge of the Self', is another prakarna. The Atman or Self, according to Shankara, is an indivisible part of the Supreme Being. Shankara describes the individual soul as the 'Self'. When self-realization is achieved, the individual soul becomes one with the Supreme Being or Brahman.

This *Atmabodha* has been composed to serve
the needs of those whose sins are removed
by austerities, who are calm, free from desire
and yearn for liberation.

Of all spiritual disciplines, self-realization is
the direct means for liberation, just as fire is
essential for cooking.

Liberation cannot be attained without
knowledge of the Self.

Knowledge alone can destroy ignorance just
as light destroys darkness.

When ignorance is destroyed,
the soul shines by itself,
as does the sun when a cloud passes.
Knowledge purifies the ignorance-stained Self
and disappears
as soap-nut-tree powder does in water.

The world is full of attachments, like a dream.
As long as the attachment exists, it appears
to be real, but it becomes unreal when one
awakens to become aware of the realization of
the Self.

Like bubbles in water, the worlds arise from,
exist in and dissolve into the Supreme Being
who is the material cause

and supporter of everything.

Diversities like caste and colour are
superimposed on the soul, just like different
flavours and colours are
superimposed upon water.

The taint of past actions is made up of the
five elements that have gone through the
process of division and combination.

Through discriminative thinking, one should
separate the pure inner Self from the
enveloping sheaths as one separates rice from
the husk by threshing with a pestle.

Though all pervading, the Self does not
manifest everywhere.
It manifests only in the intellect like a
reflection on an immaculate surface.

The Self, distinct from the body, sense

organs, mind, intellect and streams of being,
is a witness to their functions.

The Self appears to be active (in the world)
when the (five) sense organs are functioning,
just as the moon appears to be moving when
the clouds are moving.

Attachment, desire, pleasure and pain arise
when the intellect is present.
They do not exist in deep sleep when the
intellect is absent.
Hence they belong to the intellect but not to
the Self.

The Self is eternal, pure knowledge and bliss.
Just as luminosity is the nature of the sun,
coolness of water and heat of fire.

The notion of 'I know' arises from the
indiscriminate union of the existence and
intelligence of the Self and the functioning of
the intellect.

Self never undergoes modification; the
intellect is never endowed with knowledge.
Yet a man believes the two are identical and
becomes deluded
with notions of I am the knower.

Man is overcome with fear when he mistakes
himself for a living being, like a rope is
mistaken for a serpent. If one is known not
as the living being, but as the Supreme Self
one becomes free from fear.

Just as a light does not need another light to
illumine itself, similarly the Self needs no other
knowledge to make itself known, as the Self is
knowledge itself.

One should realize the oneness of the
individual Self and the Supreme Being or
Brahman through Vedic aphorisms, after
negating all those that are limited.

Visible objects like the body are born out of
ignorance and are evanescent like bubbles.
One should release the immaculate Brahman
as different from these, for 'I am Brahman'.

Shankara then defines knowledge of the Self.

I have neither birth nor old age,
nor senility or death.
I have no sense organs, nor am I attached
to sense objects.
I am distinct from the body.

Not having a mind, I have no desire, grief,
hatred or fear.
Indeed, the scriptures declare
that the Self has no mind.
It is pure.

I am without attribute and actions, eternal,
immaculate and unchanging, formless,
ever free and pure.

I pervade everything inside and outside.
I am the same in all.
I am eternal, unattached,
pure and motionless.

I am the Supreme Being which alone is
eternal, immaculate, liberated, which is one,
indivisible, non-dual, unbroken bliss, truth,
knowledge and infinity.

The innate knowledge that 'I am the
Supreme Being' destroys (mental) agitations
caused by ignorance, just like medicines
destroy diseases.

One should meditate on that one infinite
Self without any other thought,
seated in a solitary place, without any desire,
senses controlled.

The wise person should constantly meditate
upon the one Self,

as pure as the stainless sky.

There are no distinctions of knower,
knowledge and known in the Supreme Being,
because it is the sole knowledge and bliss
which shines by itself.

By constant contemplation on the Self, the
flame of knowledge is born and
burns up the entire fuel of ignorance.

As the sun rises by itself after the darkness is
destroyed by dawn,
so the Self reveals itself after ignorance is
destroyed by knowledge.

The Self is the ever-present truth.
It is not realized because of ignorance.
When ignorance is destroyed, truth seems to
be obtained
like an ornament on one's neck.

The knowledge which comes from the
realization of the Supreme Being destroys
ignorance and the ego.

An enlightened sage sees with
his eye of wisdom
the entire universe in his own self and one
Self everywhere.

The whole universe is the Supreme Being.
There exists nothing other than
the Supreme Being,
just as pots do not exist apart from clay.
The enlightened person sees everything
as the true Self.

A liberated Soul becomes Brahman (the
Supreme Being) on account of the nature of
his existence, knowledge and bliss, just as a
larva becomes a wasp.

Having crossed the ocean of delusion and

killed the demon of likes and dislikes,
the sage unites with peace, reveals himself.

The all-knowing sage is untainted by (human)
traits like the sky.
He moves unattached like the wind.

When I think of my body, I am your servant.
When I think of myself as an individual,
I am a part of you.
But when I think of you and myself,
you and I are one.

Having seen the Supreme Being, there is
nothing else to be seen.
There is no rebirth and nothing
else to be known.
Realize this in order to be the Supreme Being,
which is across, above, below, all-pervading
existence, knowledge, bliss and which is non-
dual, infinite and eternal.

Everything is united with the Supreme Being.
The Supreme Being pervades everything just
as butter pervades milk.
Realize that to be Brahman.

Pervading and illuminating the entire
universe internally and externally,
the Supreme Being shines by itself
like a red-hot ball of fire.
Brahman is everything.
If anything else is seen, it is unreal,
like a mirage.

The eye of wisdom sees the all-pervading Self
as existential consciousness.
The eye of ignorance does not see it, just as
the blind do not see the gorgeous sun.

The individual Self, heated
in the fire of knowledge,
is free from all impurities
and shines by itself like gold.

The sun of knowledge that rises in the heart,
destroys the darkness of ignorance and causes
everything to shine.

He who renounces all other activities,
worships the holy shrine within himself,
which is independent of time, space and
direction, which is present everywhere,
which is eternal bliss and stainless.
He becomes all-knowing, all-pervading and
immortal.

MOKSHA

Moksha which is liberation (from the cycle of births and deaths) is what all Hindus strive for. It is ultimate bliss and awareness. There are three paths to Consciousness, three paths to help a person focus on an entity outside his 'I' or ego. All three paths reach the same goal. Some paths take more time than others and depend on the seeker's level of intellectual maturity and the sincerity. Shankara chose the path of meditation on Advaita Vedanta as the path of intellectual enquiry.

The three paths to liberation are:

Karma Marga, the path of unselfish work or action. A spiritual seeker should act according to dharma, without being attached to the

fruits of his labour. Focused work performed
for the sake of work alone, without
permitting the ego to take ownership of the
work or experience the fruits of the work is
Karma Marga. This path is about living in
harmony with dharma. Do the right thing
because it is right.

In the Bhagavad Gita, Krishna advises:
'You have a right to perform your
prescribed duties,
but you have no right to the fruits of your action.
Never believe you are the cause of the results of
your activities,
and never be attached to not doing your duties.
Perform your duty with equal poise...giving up
attachment to success or failure,
*Such equanimity is called yoga.'**

---

*Bhagavad Gita, 2.47-28.

Bhakti Marga is the spiritual path of
devotion to a personal God with attributes
(Saguna) who is separate from the devotee.
Worshipping a phenomenon outside the ego
is known as
Bhakti Yoga. The path of devotion is for
emotional followers who worship
a particular God or Goddess of their choice.
Worshiping the divine takes one's attention
away from selfish concerns.

In the Bhagavad Gita, Krishna says:
'One can understand Me as I am, in truth, only
by devotional service.
And when one is fully conscious of Me by such
*devotion, he enters into Me thereafter.'**

Jnana Marga is the path of intellectual inquiry.
Of all paths this is the best and the most
direct path of realizing the Supreme Being.

---

*Bhagavad Gita, 18.55

Calming the mind and consciousness can be realized here and now and does not take years of transformation as required by the other paths like Karma Marga or Bhakti Marga. The other paths are recommended for people whose intellect is not mature enough for intense intellectual inquiry, for whom the path of devotion is prescribed. Jnana Marga focuses on attaining knowledge over ignorance. The path of Jnana Marga is the most difficult journey to liberation, but it is a profoundly spiritual journey.

Finally, Krishna emphasizes:
'There is nothing as sacred or comparable with knowledge (jnana).
He who is mature in yogic practice enjoys, in time, this knowledge.'*

Self-realization does not depend on any kind

---

*Bhagavad Gita, 4.39.

of consciousness.
Its nature itself is consciousness

Immortality is attained by the eternal nature
of the Soul.

One must not repeat prayers in such a way as
to make one lose
the true nature of the phrase
'Thou art that'*.

Knowledge (jnana) of the Supreme Soul leads
to instant realization.

Liberation or final release results from
knowledge.

The realization that there is but one
Supreme Soul is the aim of knowledge.

---

*Tat tvam asi

'Going to heaven' is a result of meditation
upon a personal God.
It can never be equated with the results of
meditating upon the Supreme Being
that has no attributes.

The results of rituals, like going to heaven
and so on, do not come
within one's experience.
There is reason to doubt whether
they will ever happen.
But the results of 'knowledge' lie within
human experience.

MEDITATION

Adi Shankara was a votary of meditation on the formless Supreme Being, which he discussed in several bhashyas or commentaries on the Upanishads and Bhagavad Gita.

He who seeks must meditate upon freedom
in the shrine of his heart.
The intellect cannot understand it.
It is out of the reach of thought.
It is beyond the expression of speech.

When thoughts are absent,
the present seems eternal.
When thoughts are absent,
the Self disappears.

Conquer and calm the mind.
Spiritualism does not mean passivity.
The true obstacle is desire which
disturbs the mind.
Understand and conquer it.

The meditator is not required
to cast off his ego
He may even identify with the symbol on
which he meditates.
But if the longing is not for the
Supreme Being, there is no self-realization.

The Supreme Being is unborn and formless.
Those who cannot meditate
on the Formless Being
may meditate on deities with form,
as those who meditate are full of faith.

Meditation serves to purify one's mind.
Illuminating the true nature of the world
helps to realize Advaita (non-duality).

Meditation denotes a state of mind where the
senses reject external objects.
The mind dwells on the Supreme Being
symbolized by Om,
on which the idea of the Supreme Being
is superimposed.
The single-minded person is similar to the
steady flame protected from the
draft of the wind.

One who meditates for life maintains vows
of truth, abstinence, non-injury, renunciation,
sanyasa, cleanliness, good cheer, honesty and
many other kinds of self-control, and can
be said to be one who observes the vow of
purity for life.

Greater knowledge must be realized.
Lesser knowledge must be reached
through meditation.

Ignorance disappears on realization of the
Supreme Being,
just as the darkness of the night vanishes
when the sun rises.

Ignorance causes human bondage.
So knowledge should lead to freedom.

The benefit of knowledge of Brahma is the
loss of ignorance.

Meditation on Om is a means to attain
greater and lesser knowledge.
Para, the greater knowledge, is also known as
Purusha or the Supreme.
Apara, the lower knowledge, is also known as
'prana' or the 'first-born'.

Even a righteous act (dharma) is harmful to
the seeker of liberation as it causes bondage.

One cannot both meditate and perform
rituals as the two are mutually opposite to
each other.

Knowledge and action cannot co-exist,
being opposites.
The difference between them is as between
a mountain and a mustard seed.

The Supreme Being is unborn and formless.
Ignorant devotees shrink back from the
Supreme Being.
For them the wise have given meditation with
forms and symbols.
As these are done with faith
and correct conduct,
there is little harm done by meditating
on a form.

Not all are capable of fixing their mind on
the infinite Brahman devoid of any change.

An intermediate step should not be mistaken
for the final goal.

Meditating on the great Brahman with the
aid of a symbol makes one great and wise.

In Vedanta texts, knowledge, meditation and
an act of faith all mean the same thing.
All relate to the activity and attitude
of the mind.

As the soul is subject to several births and
rebirths, it performs rituals
to reach the Gods.
These objects of worship are not one with
the Supreme Being.
The centre of the heart is the
centre for meditation,
just as the sacred saligrama is the centre for
the worship of Vishnu.

Success in meditation is achieved only when,
by intense concentration,
identity with the subject of meditation
is attained.

Meditation for the realization of the
Supreme Being
is completely within.
But even with the attainment of this, the
seed of samsara—birth, death and rebirth—
cannot be totally crushed.

One who is pure realizes the inner self.

One must not repeat prayers so as to lose the
true meaning of the verse.
If ideas arise that 'I must do this', 'I am
competent to do this', 'it is my duty to do this',
then wrong notions of Brahman arise.

Knowledge of the Supreme Being
leads to immediate realization.
The realization that there is but one
Supreme Being
is the aim of all knowledge.

Meditation alone cannot end rebirth.
When a person realizes that he does not go
anywhere because he has nowhere to go,
he has achieved self-realization.

Since self-realization is immediate, there is no
need to fear about getting the result.
By doing rituals, whose results—like attaining
heaven—do not come in a lifetime,
there is reason to doubt whether they will
ever happen or not.

By meditating on Brahman with qualities,
one obtains ascendancy and freedom from sin.
But knowledge of the unqualified Brahman
gives rise to the awareness that

'I am Brahman'*, neither doer nor enjoyer.
He who knows Brahman knows that he was
never an actor or enjoyer
in the past, present or future.

An intense desire for the realization of the
Supreme Being
is the only means of attaining Brahman.

Meditation is the continuous flow of similar
ideas unmixed by any dissimilar ideas.
Meditation is keeping up a continuous flow
of the same idea,
without any break by another idea.
Visualize the object of meditation, dwell on it
for a long time,
continuously and unbroken, like a flowing
thread of oil.

*Aham Brahmasmi

Meditation is also a ritual.

When you meditate, you successfully change
your mental state.
Then a superior state comes about.

Greatness is attained by meditation.

Through meditation,
one conquers evil actions.

SPIRITUAL PRACTICE

Adi Shankara wrote five verses—*Sadhana Panchakam*—giving advice on spiritual practice. It is a simple handbook for a person entering the life of a yogi or sanyas. Today it is relevant for any seeker to better understand the path of spiritual practice.

Seek friendship with wise men.
Be firmly devoted to the Lord.
Cultivate the virtue of peace.
Eschew all action motivated by desire.
Find the perfect teacher.
Meditate on Om.

Study the Vedas every day.
Perform your duties diligently.

Dedicate all your actions to the Lord.
Renounce all desire for the pleasures of
material objects, which are riddled with pain.
Seek the Supreme Being constantly.

Reflect on the meaning of the Upanishads,
take refuge in the Truth of Brahman.
Avoid perverse arguments, but follow the
unbiased logic of revealed works.
Always be absorbed in the knowledge that
'I am Brahman'.
Renounce pride.
Give up the misconception that
'I am the body'.
Give up totally the tendency to
argue with the wise.

Diseases are treated by hunger.
Beg for your food every day.
Live contentedly with whatever comes to your
lot, as ordained.
Endure all opposites: heat and cold, and so on.

Avoid useless speech.
Save yourself from becoming enmeshed in
people's kindness.

Live happily in solitude.
Concentrate in silence on the
Supreme Being.
Realize and see the all-pervading Soul
everywhere.
Recognize that the finite Universe is a
projection of the Soul.
Conquer the effects of the deeds of an earlier
life by right action in this life.
Through wisdom become detached from
future actions.
Experience and exhaust the fruits
of past actions.
Thereafter, live absorbed in the knowledge
that 'I am Brahman'!

RITUALS

Contrary to popular belief, Shankara asserted that the world was real. If the body is real, so is the world, he said. The world is a fact before one realizes Brahman. The body and the world come and go together. After experiencing the Supreme Being, the world and the body cease to exist. What, then, is the use of rituals to attain worldly desires, when truth is knowledge of the Supreme Being?

Shankara had intensive arguments with the followers of Mimamsa (founded by the scholar Jaimini) who believed in the importance of rituals for attaining heaven. He divided them into four categories: daily rituals (nitya karma), which do not produce any fruit; rituals performed on special occasions (naimittika karma) like on the full moon, new moon, eclipses, etc.; rituals performed to achieve special desires (kamya karma) like the birth of a son, etc.; and prohibited rituals (pratishiddha karma), the performance of which will result in evil. Shankara used the word karma for rituals, leading to much confusion, for karma can also be used for action. He advocated spiritual action rather than ritualistic action.

Shankara believed that the Vedas revealed the means to an end and was ambiguous about their adoption. He condemned rituals as completely useless for spiritual evolution. It was necessary, advocated Shankara, to outgrow rituals, for they led to human bondage, not liberation.

When heaven does not exist,
what is the point of rituals?

As ignorance causes bondage,
so knowledge produces freedom.

Before attaining realization of the
Supreme Being,

we should regard our worldly activities
as real,
Just as dreams seem real to us
till we wake up.

Happiness comes from the
freedom of the senses.
While there is thirst for pleasure there can be
no true happiness.
Desire for worldly objects leads to misery.

The rituals suggested by the scriptures are
intended for the unenlightened.

When a person achieves knowledge, he ceases
to perform rituals.

He who does not yearn for material
possessions and does not desire anything else
because he has acquired knowledge of the
Supreme Truth, he is firm in his knowledge.
These are the attributes of the true yogin,

who seeks liberation from all attributes and
characteristics.

People may quote the scriptures and offer
prayers to the gods;
they may perform rituals and worship deities.
But no liberation will be secured
by these methods.
Only identification with the Supreme Being
will obtain liberation.

One may go to the Ganga and to different
oceans for a dip,
one may do penance and charity,
but people who do not have right knowledge
and mindlessly repeat these rituals assuming
that they alone will help them,
they can never get liberation, irrespective of
which religion they may belong to.

On realization of the Supreme Being,
darkness disappears,

just as on the appearance of the sun,
night disappears.

Realization of Brahman is the means to the
highest realms of life,
which is within the reach of all mortals.

Supreme happiness comes from Dharma,
which is steady devotion to the
Supreme Soul, preceded by renunciation of
all rituals.

The Bhagavad Gita teaches that he who has
acquired knowledge of the Supreme Being
should renounce desire, not perform rituals.

Identifying the soul with the body
is the core of ignorance.
Right knowledge leads to a cessation of the
cycle of birth, death and rebirth.

The ignorant man who longs for results
performs rituals.

What is the object of rituals like worship,
gifts and offering oblations to fire?
Illogical knowledge is surrounded by
ignorance.
Ignorant mortals are deluded and think,
'I act, I cause to act, I shall enjoy,
I cause to enjoy.'

Rituals based on illusion are impossible
for a realized Soul.

Those who perform rituals are unenlightened
ritualists, in spite of their great devotion.

If a person is unable to achieve the yoga of
meditation, he may perform rituals.

If daily rituals prescribed by the Vedas do not
produce results, they have no purpose.

It is not possible for a man of knowledge to
have knowledge and perform rituals at the

same time as they are incompatible
with each other.
If you aspire for liberation, renounce rituals.

Even Dharma or righteous conduct can cause
bondage to a seeker for liberation (moksha).

Meditation in which there is no distinction
between Knowledge and the Supreme Being
is not appropriate for a person
in search of rituals.

Renounce desire, and the means to attain
desire, which consist of rituals.

KNOWLEDGE

The Vedas, said Shankara, reveal and do not command. Unlike other religious teachers, he based his propositions on ordinary experience. The only Vedic proposition he believed in absolutely was the oneness of the Soul with the Supreme Being.

Perception cannot be challenged because it
has been perceived.
Perception cannot be nullified by inference.

Perception and memory are movements of
the mind.

The senses are the means of knowledge, and
each is powerful in its own sphere.

The scope of one is not the scope
of the other.

When knowledge arises, like the light of the
sun, illusion or maya is removed.
There is the realization that the Supreme Being
is without beginning or end...
without birth or death or decay,
and is fearless.

A person whose body is placed in the sun
erroneously thinks
that the body has the properties of light.
Similarly, he looks upon the intellect as the
Supreme Being.

An ignorant man differentiates between
the body, mind and intellect.
He does not know that he is a part of the
Supreme Being.

Pain arises from identifying oneself

with the body.
By not identifying oneself with the body,
one is free from pain.

Just as the heat of the sun in a part of the
body is known to the sufferer
similarly, pain, pleasure and the intellect are
the objects of the Supreme.

Knowledge does not stay after the
removal of duality.
The removal of self-consciousness is
simultaneous with the operation of valid
knowledge.

I have no eyes so I cannot see,
I have no auditory organ, so I cannot hear,
I have no organ of speech so how can I speak?
I have no mind, so how can I think?

There are three things that are rare and
obtained by Divine Grace alone:

human birth, a burning longing for liberation
and the protective care of a perfect saint.

Among the means conducive to liberation,
devotion holds the supreme place.
It is only by Divine Grace that the aspiration
for knowledge of Advaita arises.

People do not receive self-knowledge on
account of the fear that it might
shake their routine,
like Udanka who refused to accept genuine
nectar thinking that it was urine.

All-pervading like ether,
I have no hunger, thirst, grief, delusion, old
age or death,
For I am without a body.

The Vedas tell us that actions produced by
desire caused by ignorance
give perishable results.

I have neither knowledge nor ignorance
as I am the eternal Consciousness.

The Knowledge of the Knower is eternal,
pure, infinite and without another.

He who knows the reality of the
Supreme Being becomes successful
in attaining his goal and achieving perfection.
A Knower of Brahman becomes Brahman.

There is no other attainment higher than
that of the Supreme Being.
That is the purpose of the teachings of the
Vedas and Smritis.

The Supreme Being does not depend on
anything else in order to be acquired.

Control the body with austerities
to purify the mind.

Oh Lord, when shall I be free of this cycle of
repeated births and deaths?

Knowledge of Brahman cannot be acquired
by any means other than enquiry.
Enquiry is like the light that is indispensable
to view objects.

Who am I? How is this world created?
Of what material is this world made?

Wisdom dispels darkness.
Ignorance is darkness.

The unreal has no existence and the real
never ceases to be.

Freedom is obtained only through our own
eyes, once they have been opened by insight,
never through the eyes of another.
Through our own eyes we learn what the
moon looks like.

How can we learn this through the
eyes of others?*
The Self does not act, but on it is
superimposed the consciousness of actions
and their fruits.
These superimpositions are
removed by the realization
of the non-dual Supreme Being (Advaita).

The highest Supreme is the object of right
viewing, right knowledge and right intuition**.

Self-realization does not depend on any type
of consciousness.
It is consciousness or awareness of the Self.

Immortality is attained by the eternal nature
of the Individual Soul.

---

*Shankara's Crest Jewel of Discrimination: Viveka-Chudamani, Swami
Prabhavananda and Christopher Isherwood (trs.), Vedanta Press,
1970, p. 40.
**Samyag darshana, the right faith or faith in the fundamentals.

If immortality were produced by knowledge,
it will be non-eternal,
such as the result of a ritual or an activity.
Knowledge removes identification with the
non-Self.

MAYA

Maya or illusion is the non-apprehension of truth and a dream state of misapprehension. The world, said Shankara, is maya or illusion. There is no duality separating the individual soul from the Supreme Soul. This non-duality is the highest form of reality. Maya or illusion causes us to perceive duality where there is unity.

Maya is the cause of delusion.

Maya evolves into the three states of waking,
dreaming and deep sleep.
The Supreme Being, though only one,
appears to be many,
like the reflections of the sun on water.

What is perceived in waking is contradicted
in a dream state.
Hence we think it is unreal, just as things
perceived in a dream state.

Even as a mirage is unreal, so too are the
novel things perceived in a dream.
These are features of the perceiver alone and
so are unreal.

In the dream state, the internal and external
are illusory.
The distinction between the real and non-real
is untrue.

The Soul by its own maya imagines different
objects within itself.
Waking objects are also imagined, just like
dream objects.

The things perceived in waking are illusory.
They do not exist in the beginning, middle

or end, like a mirage.

When realization of the truth of the
Supreme Being is established, then knowledge
is established in the Supreme.
The mind appears as a duality consisting of
the teacher and the taught, through maya.
Even in waking, the mind
moves through maya.
The Supreme Being alone is constant.

The duality which is called the world
is mere illusion.
Non-duality is the supreme truth.
Hence no world either as evolving or
dissolving exists.

All the talk of pupil, teacher and sacred texts
is for the sake of teaching.
When the aim of teaching, namely knowledge
of the Supreme Truth, has been gained,
there is no duality.

When maya is taught by a guru who knows
the truth of Vedanta,
the individual soul realizes that it is neither
cause nor effect.

By reasoning it is possible to establish that
duality is an illusion.

The Supreme Soul is both cause and effect.
Because the individual soul has not been
known as distinct from the present world of
misery, the Supreme Soul is imagined to be
different as different beings.
He who knows that other than the Soul,
imagined things have no existence,
understands the meaning of the Veda.
He who does not know the Self cannot
comprehend the Veda.

This universe of duality is unreal.
Duality is unreal, a pure imagination
of the mind.

The Self is supreme and non-dual.
Non-duality is fearless and therefore
auspicious.

Why is non-duality auspicious?
When the individual soul is of the nature of
the supremely real Self
nothing exists as non-separate
as nothing is real.
Therefore non-duality alone is auspicious

PERSONAL EFFORT

Personal effort (purushakara), not rituals, is necessary for self-control and self-realization, not rituals, said Shankara.

> When the source of evil is known, exert
> yourself to destroy it.

> Strive hard and suppress the senses,
> by controlling your nature,
> practicing compassion and non-violence.

> A person whose mind is controlled by desire
> and hate cannot achieve knowledge.
> A person whose mind is controlled by
> passion cannot obtain knowledge of the

Supreme Being, since there are many
obstacles in his path.

Good and evil are not absolute but depend
on each one's opinion.

There cannot be alternatives to truth.
There can be alternatives in rituals and
actions.

If there is no ambit for personal effort,
then the scriptures would be useless.

He who follows the scriptures should rise
above his likes and dislikes.
The nature of a person determines the course
of his actions, motivated by likes and dislikes.
When a person restrains his likes and
dislikes, he is no longer controlled by nature.

Brahman exists. It is eternal.
There should be a desire to know it.

It does not depend on rituals.

Knowledge of Brahman
does not depend on rituals.
When an on object is near the eye,
the eye sees it.
So also the knowledge of Brahman.

There is no alternative to truth, such as 'it is
so' or 'it is not so', or 'it is' or 'it is not'.

True knowledge does not depend on mental
activity, it depends on the object.
Similarly, the knowledge of Brahman depends
on the nature of Brahman,
who is an existing Being.

Knowledge depends on the knower.
So Atman has to be situated before
knowledge of Atman commences.

Knowledge is acquired through cognition.

So cognition is happiness.

Knowledge and ignorance are objects of
perception within the mind.

The mere word does not constitute reality.
The word is different from the object which
it denotes.

TRUE NATURE OF THE SELF

Adi Shankara sums up the essence of his beliefs—or
rather, the negation of them—in the *Dasha shloki*. He
says that relationships, symbols and manifestations are
maya and only the Atman or the Supreme Brahman
is real. As in the Upanishads, Shankara emphasizes
that only the person who realizes the Self transcends
worldly sorrow.

In form and theme, the *Dasha shloki* appears
similar to the *Atma shloki*. But the two are very
different, and even in contrast to each other. In the
Dasha shloki, Shankara abjures much more than he did
in the *Atma shloki*. For example, he mentions caste in
the *Dasha shloki*: this could only have happened after
his encounter with the Chandala in Kashi. He also
abjures the various sects. It could be that the *Atma*

shloki encompassed Shankara's philosophy when he was a young man and the *Dasha shloki* was his last pronouncement on the non-dual nature of the Atman. Thus when Shankara's disciples asked him, towards the end of his life, what a devotee should do in order follow to achieve jnana or self-realization, his answer was the *Dasha shloki* or *Nirvana dashakam*.

I am not the earth, water, fire, air or ether,
or anything related to the body,
I am not the faculties individually or in total,
I am one with Brahman in deep sleep.
I am the residue, the auspicious,
the only One, I am Shiva.

I have no caste nor duties attached to caste,
I am not concentration, meditation, or yoga,
For the mistaken senses of I and mine, the
body and mind have been abandoned.
I am the residue, the auspicious,
the only One, I am Shiva.

I have no mother, nor father,
no gods nor region,
I know no scriptures, no rituals, no sacred
places, say the sages,
for, in the state of deep sleep,
all these are negated
and that state is completely devoid
(of any perception).
I am the residue, the auspicious,
the only One, I am Shiva.

There is no Sankhya no Shaiva, nor
Pancharatra nor Jaina.
The concept of the Mimamsaka and others
does not exist,
for, through direct realization of what is
qualified, the Self is known as
absolutely pure.
I am the residue, the auspicious,
the only One, I am Shiva.

There is neither above nor below, neither

inside nor outside,
no middle nor across,
no east or west direction.
For it is all pervasive like space. It is not
parted, it is homogeneous in nature.
I am the residue, the auspicious,
the only One, I am Shiva.

I am neither white nor black,
neither red nor yellow,
neither dwarfish nor stout,
neither short nor long.
I am shapeless, in the nature of light,
I am the residue, the auspicious,
the only One, I am Shiva.

There is neither ruler nor rules,
no pupil nor teaching,
There is no you or I. This universe is not,
for realization of the true nature of the
Supreme Being does not tolerate any distinction.
I am the residue, the auspicious,

the only One, I am Shiva.

There is no waking for me, no dream,
no deep sleep,
I am not conditioned by these three states,
I am the fourth state of bliss
beyond these three.
I am the residue, the auspicious,
the only One, I am Shiva.

All this universe other than the
Supreme Being is unreal,
the Supreme Being alone is all inclusive,
constitutes the Ultimate Reality.
It is self-established and self-dependant.
I am the residue, the auspicious,
the only One, I am Shiva.

It is One, for how can there be
a distinct second?
It is not absolute, nor non-absolute,
it is neither void nor non-void. It does not

admit of a duality.

How then can I speak about that which is
established by all the Upanishads?

THE OCEAN OF NECTAR

The *Viveka Chudamani* is a massive and authoritative work of 580 verses that combines Shankara's conviction with his brilliant analysis. (Included here are some of the verses.) Shankara says that we must discriminate between Brahman, who alone is real, and the universe that is unreal, between the permanent and the transient. For Shankara, liberation—moksha, mukti or nirvana—was the ultimate loosening of the bonds of birth, death and rebirth and merging with the Supreme Being or Brahman.

One who can distinguish between the real
and the unreal,
whose mind turns away from
the unreal and is calm,

and longs for liberation
is alone qualified to seek the Supreme Being.

First comes discrimination between
the real and the unreal,
next comes an aversion to the enjoyment of
the fruits of one's action,
then comes calmness,
and finally comes the yearning for liberation.

A firm conviction that the Supreme Being is
real and the world is unreal
is described as the discrimination between the
real and the unreal.

Three things are indeed rare and are due to
the grace of God:
a human birth, a longing for liberation and
the protection of a perfect sage.

The conviction of Truth comes from
reasoning upon

the salutary counsel of the wise,
not by bathing in the sacred waters,
nor by gifts nor by hundreds of pranayamas.

Maya or illusion is made up
of the three gunas.
It is she who brings forth
this whole universe.

Lust, anger, avarice, arrogance, spite,
egoism, envy and jealousy
are the dire attributes of rajas (guna).
Therefore rajas is a cause of bondage.

Ignorance, lassitude, dullness, sleep,
inadvertence and stupidity
are attributes of tamas (guna).
One tied to this does not
comprehend anything.

Pure sattva (guna) is clear like water.
The traits of sattva are absence of pride,
purity, contentment, non-killing, truthfulness,
faith, devotion, yearning for liberation, divine

tendencies and turning away from the unreal.

Where renunciation and the yearning for
freedom are tepid,
calmness and other practices are like the
mirage of water in the desert.

It is in the nature of the
magnanimous to help others.
Like the moon who
voluntarily saves the earth
from the flaming rays of the sun.

The transparent truth about the soul, which
is hidden by the effects of maya or illusion,
may be attained through the instructions of
one who knows the Supreme Being.
This may be followed by
reflection and meditation,
but not by perverted arguments.

The first step to liberation is to develop an

aversion to all perishable matter,
then follows calmness, self-control,
forbearance and all motivated work.

Now I am going to tell you of the real nature
of the Paramatma (Supreme Being):
Who knows everything that happens in the
waking state,
in dream and in profound sleep,
is aware of the presence or absence of the
mind and its functions.
This is He.

Who sees all, but whom nobody can see,
who illumines the mind but whom they
cannot illumine.
This is He.

By whom this universe is pervaded, but
whom nothing pervades,
And all the universe shines as His reflection.
This is He.

The Atman (Soul) is neither born nor dies, it
neither grows nor decays,
nor does it undergo any change,
for it is eternal.
It does not cease to exist even when this
body is destroyed,
for it is independent.

Of the tree of samsara (existence),
ignorance is the seed,
the body is the sprout,
attachment its tender leaves, work its water,
the body its trunk,
the vital forces its branches
the organs its twigs, the sense-objects its
flowers, misery its fruits,
and the individual soul
is the bird seated upon it.

Just as stone, tree, grass, paddy and husk,
when burnt, are reduced to ashes,
the whole universe comprising the body,

organs, life-giving force and mind,
when burnt by the fire of realization,
is reduced to the Supreme Self.

As darkness vanishes in the sun's radiance,
so the whole universe is merged in the
Supreme Being.

When a jar is broken, the space enclosed by
it becomes the limitless space.
So when the limitations are destroyed, the
knower of Brahman becomes Brahman itself.

As milk poured into milk, oil into oil and
water into water becomes one with it,
similarly, the wise one who has realized
the Supreme Being becomes one with the
Supreme Being.

There is neither death nor birth, neither a
bound nor a struggling soul,
neither a seeker after liberation

nor a liberated one.
This is the ultimate truth.

We alone can get rid of the bondage caused
by the fetters of ignorance
desire and action even in
a hundred crore kalpas.

Neither by Yoga*, nor by Samkhya**,
nor by work*** nor by learning,
but by realization of one's identity
with the Supreme Being
is liberation possible, and by no other means.

Loud speech, consisting of a shower of words,
skill in expounding the scriptures and similar
erudition merely bring personal enjoyment to
the scholar but are no good for liberation.

---

*Hatha yoga for the body.
**A school of philosophy which believes in a sentient Purusha
and an active Prakriti.
***Work to achieve material ends.

The disciple asks his master:
What is bondage? How has it come about,
how does it continue to exist and how is one
free from it?
What is the non-Self and who is the
Supreme Being?
And how can one discriminate between them?

The teacher replies:
You are blessed. You have achieved your life's end
and sanctified your family,
Now you wish to attain Brahmanhood by
freeing yourself
from the bondage of ignorance.

Resting the mind on the Supreme Being,
after detaching it from sense-objects
by continuous observation of their defects,
is called saama or calmness.

Turning sense-organs away from sense subjects
is called daama or self-control.
The best form of self-withdrawal is when the mind

ceases to be influenced by external objects.

I have revealed this excellent and profound
secret which is the message of Vedanta,
the crown of the Vedas,
considering that you aspire for liberation and
have a mind free of desire.

For those who are afflicted
by burning pain due to misery,
and who through delusion wander about the
desert in search of water,
for them here is the triumphant message of
Shankara, pointing out, within easy reach,
the comforting ocean of nectar, Brahman,
the One without a second,
to lead them to liberation.